THE BOOK TO HAVE WHEN GOOD
COOKING GOES BAD...

FIXES

*PROBLEM SOLVING,
SUBSTITUTIONS, & MORE*

BY SUZANNE MAXWELL
AND SHARON PULTE

Visit us at www.fastfixes.net

Printed By:

ISBN 13: 9781495909757

Library of Congress Control Number: 2014902890
CreateSpace Independent Publishing Platform
North Charleston, South Carolina

Contents

CONTENTS

CHAPTER ONE

Fast Fixes

MORNINGS MATTER
Eggs
Pancakes and Waffles
Breakfast Grains
Bread
Coffee, Tea

AND THE DAY GOES ON
Salads
Fruit
Vegetables
Starches
Sauce 101
Tips about Butter and Oils
How to Handle Your Spices
Cheese Basics
Meats, Poultry, and Seafood
Desserts: from Chocolate to Meringue

MORNINGS MATTER

Eggs

· ·

Basics

» Does size matter in eggs? Yes! Extra large eggs are, well, larger.

» Always use large eggs unless the recipe calls for a different size.

» Is It Fresh? Place the egg in a jar of water. If the egg lies on its side, it is very fresh. If the egg floats, it is bad! If the egg lies upright in the jar, it is still OK to eat, but eat it quickly!

Boiled/Hard-Cooked Eggs: Place eggs in a single layer in a saucepan. Add water to a depth of 3 inches, just covering the eggs, and bring to a rolling boil. Cover pan and remove from heat. Let stand for 12 minutes. Drain and fill pan with cold water for a few minutes to cool eggs. To peel hard-cooked eggs, drain out the water, shake the pan back and forth to crack the shells!

Perfect Scrambled Eggs: Combine eggs with a splash of half-and-half, and whisk well. Use a 10-inch skillet to create a thick layer of eggs. Start the egg mixture over medium-high heat. When the eggs start to coagulate, turn the heat to low and finish cooking. Add bits of butter to uncooked eggs. This helps to make scrambled eggs and omelets creamier.

Best Spices for Eggs: Basil, chervil, chili, chives, curry, dill, fennel, ginger, marjoram, oregano, paprika, parsley, sage, tarragon, and thyme.

» We recommend using no more than two herbs at a time plus salt and pepper.

Fixes

Runny Poached Eggs: Add 1 tablespoon vinegar to the water—this will help keep the eggs intact and not affect the taste.

Perfect Pancakes and Waffles

Basics

» Don't overmix; leave the lumps in!

» Don't skimp on the baking soda; it's a browning and rising booster.

» Let the batter rest for 10 minutes before cooking.

» Cooking for a crowd? Keep cooked pancakes in a 200°F oven on a wire rack while you continue to cook.

Fixes

Need Fluffier Pancakes and Waffles? Separate the eggs. First, fold the yolks into the batter. Next, whip the whites until medium peaks form, and then gently fold into the batter. You can even try replacing all or some of the liquid in the recipe with a carbonated beverage.

Are Your Waffles a Bit Soft? For crispy waffles, use a recipe that calls for cornstarch.

Undercooked Pancakes? Make sure you have bubbles on the surface of your pancakes before you flip them. Also, cook a test pancake with 1 tablespoon of batter to make sure the griddle is at the right temperature.

Breakfast Grains

. . . .

Basics

» **To Toast or Not to Toast:**
Toasting the oats prior to
cooking adds a rich, nutty
flavor. Simply toast oats in
a little melted butter over
medium heat until brown.
Cook as you prefer.

Steel-Cut, Irish, Scottish, and Pinhead Oatmeal: All are similar.
Add oats to lightly salted, boiling water. Turn the heat off, and then
soak overnight. In the morning, simply warm the oats over medium-
low heat and enjoy.

» If you don't have time to soak them overnight, boil the oats in
water and simmer for about 30 minutes. Try not to stir them too
often. Less stirring = more texture.

Hominy Grits and Cornmeal: Finely milled, dried corn kernels
are best if poured into rapidly boiling water (1 cup grain to 4 cups
water) and then cooked gently for approximately 20 minutes.

Rolled Oats: Cook oats in plenty of salted, boiling water until they
are tender enough to bite through but retain some texture, about 5
minutes. Once cooked, strain them and rinse under hot water.

Granola vs. Muesli: Granola = grains toasted before adding other
ingredients. Muesli = grains mixed raw. Both may contain some or
all of the following: varieties of wheat; millet; amaranth; or rolled,

steel-cut, or quick oats. These grains may be processed and rolled into flakes, cracked as in bulgur wheat, or ground into flour. You may also find quinoa or buckwheat in these cereals.

Kasha: Another type of cereal, generally containing buckwheat groats, but it may contain millet, barley, wheat, or oats. Check your ingredients. Place ¼ cup Kasha in a pan and cover with 1 cup water or broth. Bring to a boil and then simmer for approximately 10 minutes or until tender.

> GROAT: THE HULLED GRAIN OF VARIOUS CEREALS, SUCH AS OAT, WHEAT, AND RYE.

Need Gluten Free or Low-Gluten Cereal or Bread? Look for sorghum flour, brown rice flour, white rice flour, corn flour, millet flour, certified gluten-free flour, and teff. These grains contain little or no gluten.

Bread

Bread Basics

» To determine if dough has doubled in bulk, lightly press two fingers into dough. If a dent remains, the dough has doubled.

» Salt is essential. Don't skip it in an effort to lower sodium; you will lower taste.

» Keep unused yeast in the freezer, and be sure to check the expiration date.

» Some bread does not require a sponge or yeast starter step. It's great for rustic breads, but that's about it.

» Use a stand mixer to knead; it takes less effort and it is faster. Too much kneading leads to flavor loss, so be careful!

» Follow rising times.

» It is best to use a nonshiny pan.

» For a crusty top, brush loaves halfway through baking with a solution of 1 teaspoon salt and ½ cup water.

Best Spices for Breads: Anise, basil, caraway, cardamom, cinnamon, coriander, cumin, dill, garlic, lemon peel, orange peel, oregano, poppy seeds, rosemary, saffron, sage, and thyme. We recommend using only one spice or using complimentary spices, such as poppy seed and lemon peel.

Flours and Yeasts

Bread Flour: Made with "hard" winter wheat, which has a high gluten content. It will rise a bit more than all-purpose flour.

» **Hard Wheat:** Hard wheat kernels high in gluten.

» **Soft Wheat:** Soft wheat kernels, usually high in starch but low in gluten.

All-Purpose Flour: Made with a combination of "hard" and "soft" wheat, has less gluten than bread flour, and will rise slightly less than bread flour.

Self-Rising Flour: Includes all-purpose flour, salt, and baking powder.

Cake Flour: Made from "soft" wheat, has less gluten, and will provide a light airy texture.

Active Dry Yeast: To proof yeast, dissolve it in ¼ cup warm water (105°F to 110°F).

» When using compressed cake yeast, the proofing liquid should be 80°F to 90°F. Note the difference between proofing compressed and active yeasts.

» You can proof, or test, active dry yeast to make sure it's still good by simply stirring 1 teaspoon of sugar into the dissolved yeast. If it doubles in volume in 10 minutes, then it is still good!

Fast-Rising Yeast: Also known as bread machine yeasts. These contain ascorbic acid and you can add them directly to flour. There is no need to proof this type of yeast, but the bread or dough may not rise as much as it would with active dry yeast.

Fixes

Did the Bread Fall in the Oven or Not Rise? Old yeast or the type of yeast you are using can also be the cause. Also note that yeast can die in water that is too hot or cold or from rising in a location that is too cool.

Does My Bread Taste Too Yeasty? Perhaps the bread rose too long, and/or the location of the rising was too warm.

The Bread Is Too Thick, Heavy, or Dense: You may have used too much flour; check your recipe. Note: flours such as whole wheat and rye produce denser breads. Or, the dough needed more kneading, the rising period was too long, or the oven temperature was too low. Check your recipe.

Not Browning: The pan may be too shiny (a metal pan) or the pan may not be placed in the oven correctly. Put the pan in the middle of the oven on the middle rack.

The Top of the Loaf Is Cracked: Did you cool the bread in a drafty place? If so, that could be the culprit. Or it may be that you did not mix the dough well.

Crumbly Bread: You may not have kneaded the dough long enough, you may have used too much flour, the rising place may have been too warm, you may have let the bread rise too long, or the oven temperature could have been too low. Check your recipe and try again.

The Bread Is Not Done on the Bottom: Remember to remove the bread from the pan and let it cool on a rack. This will ensure adequate cooking.

Check Your Water

Soft Water: Water without minerals can make dough sticky and soggy.

Hard Water: Minerals in hard water can affect the color and sometimes the taste of your foods, as well as make the fermentation of yeasts take longer.

» To determine if you have hard water, fill a plastic bottle half full with water. Add a few drops of liquid soap, place cap on, and shake the bottle. If when you remove the cap, the bottle overflows, you do not have hard water. If the bubbles are slow forming or only a few bubbles form, then you may have hard water.

Do You Have Extremely Hard or Soft Water? If so, use bottled water while cooking items such as bread, cakes, etc.

Coffee and Tea

Perhaps the Most Important Part of Every Day

Coffee Basics

» Use loose
beans and
grind them as
needed—this
really is the
key to great
coffee!

» A coffee burr grinder is the best option for whole beans.

» Don't buy preground beans. You will be disappointed in the
flavor, especially if you really want to impress.

» Remember to check the expiration date on the package.

» Remember, if it says dark roast, it means strong coffee. The
darker the roast, the stronger the coffee.

» If you're feeling fancy and want to pull out that plunger pot
you rarely use, be sure to use coarse ground coffee for the best
taste.

Fixes

Flavor a Bit Off? You may have underroasted beans. Sorting through the beans and picking out the very pale or green beans should improve the taste.
» If hard water affects the coffee taste, use filtered, boiled, or bottled water for a perfect cup every time.

» To keep the pot clean, rinse it daily and wash it weekly with soapy water to remove the coffee oil residue.

Tea Basics

» *For the perfect cup* use 6 oz. of fresh, fully boiled water poured over 1 teaspoon of tea leaves.

> THERE IS ONLY ONE TEA PLANT SPECIES! AND IT IS OF THE "CAMELLIA" FAMILY. ALL VARIETIES ARE HARVESTED FROM THIS ONE SPECIES.

Black and Herbal Teas: Brew with water that is between 208°F and 212°F.
» Black tea is allowed to ferment for a certain period of time after plucking. The tea is then rolled and dried until it has the familiar "tea" smell.

13

Oolong Tea: Brew with water that is between 180°F and 190°F.

» Created similarly to green and black teas but the leaves are never rolled.

Green and White Teas: These are very delicate teas. Use water that is slightly cooled to between 170°F and 185°F.

» Green tea is allowed to wither and dry immediately after plucking. It is then rolled into tea leaves.

» White tea is created from new tea leaf buds then allowed to wither and dry. It is mild and somewhat sweet.

Fixes

Tea Flavor a Bit Off? Make sure all ingredients are listed. If the list simply says "herbs," the taste may surprise you!

Bitter Tea? Check the blend of tea leaves. It may be that your water is too hot for the leaves, and you have "burned" the leaves instead of steeping them.

AND THE DAY GOES ON

Salads

. . . .

Salad Basics

» Select fresh produce with limited or no bruising.

» Dirt is good on root vegetables. Potatoes with a bit of dirt tend to last longer.

» Avoid cutting or trimming the vegetable until you need it. Excess air exposure will speed up the deterioration.

» Excess light can promote sprouting, so keep vegetables in a dark place.

» Don't refrigerate your tomatoes. They lose their flavor and texture quickly!

Best Spices for Salads: Basil, caraway seeds, chives, dill, garlic, lemon peel, marjoram, mint, oregano, parsley, rosemary, tarragon, and thyme.

Keep That Guacamole Green: To store avocado dips and sauces, add the avocado seed to the finished dip/sauce and store covered in the refrigerator. The seed will help to stall the reaction that causes avocados to brown when exposed to air. Remove before serving, and enjoy a greener dip!

Chopping Celery: Instead of breaking off one rib at a time, try chopping the whole stalk. It's easier, gets you the amount you need, and shortens the stalk for easier storage! Don't forget to toss it in the salad spinner to wash.

Seeding Tomatoes: Try using your salad spinner! Just chop the tomatoes in smaller chunks and spin away, the seeds should release easily.

Tomatillos: To check for ripeness they should be firm, not soft like tomatoes, with skin intact and no bruising. Store in the refrigerator once ripe and enjoy raw or cooked. Cooking brings out the sweet flavor for salsas and chutneys.

Edible Flowers: These are fun for salads and yummy to eat! Try borage, pansy, nasturtium, calendula, rosemary, fennel, squash, and chive blossoms.

Fruits

. . . .

Apples
What Apples to Use When...

Pies	Crisp	Apple Sauce	Cake
Braeburn	Cortland	Braeburn	Braeburn
Cameo	Granny Smith	Cameo	Bramley
Crispin	Honey Crisp	Cortland	Granny Smith
Cortland	Jonagold	Crispin	Honey Crisp
Empire		Fuji	Ida Red
Ida Red		Gala	Jonathon
Granny Smith		Golden Delicious	Pink Lady
Jonathan		Ida Red	
Mutsu		Jonagold	
Northern Spy		Jonathon	
Pippin		McIntosh	
Pink Lady		Mutsu	
		Pink Lady	
		Rome	

Apples for Batters and Doughs: When using fresh apples for batters, microwave apples for a minute or two before adding for a soft, tender product.

Dried Apples: Cover with boiling water until tender, then drain, pat dry.

> THERE ARE HUNDREDS OF VARIETIES OF APPLES.
> IT'S BEST TO FOLLOW YOUR RECIPE IF POSSIBLE.

Bananas: Peel them from the bottom and you won't have to pick off the strings.

» Take the bananas apart when you get home from the store. If you leave them connected, they ripen faster.

» Keep your bananas in the refrigerator—the skins turn brown, but they stay firm longer.

Grapefruit, Melon, Orange, and Peach Varieties: There are several varieties of each type of fruit. For the most part, you can use any variety of grapefruit, melon, orange, or peach in a recipe.

Mango: Hold a mango on a cutting surface, stem end up. With a paring knife, carefully cut the mango into two halves and separate from pit. Score the inside of each half and gently push the skin side out. Cut the cubes off the skin.

Papaya: Hold a papaya on its side and slice in half lengthwise. Scoop out seeds and use as a garnish (start with a small amount of 1 teaspoon to make sure you can tolerate them). Place cut side down and peel. Remove 1 to 3 inches from the narrow end, slice, and enjoy! The seeds are known to be great for digestive health and can be eaten raw.

Pears

Eating/Poaching	Pies	Muffins/Breads	Canning
Anjou	Anjou	Anjou	Bartlett
Asian	Bartlett	Bartlett	Bosc
Bartlett	Bosc	Bosc	Forelle
Bosc	Forelle	Comice	Nelis
Comice	Nelis	Forelle	Seckel
Forelle		Nelis	
Nelis		Seckel	
Seckel			

Don't refrigerate an unripe pear. It will continue to ripen as it sits at room temperature.

Best Spices for Most Fruits: Allspice, anise, cardamom, cinnamom, cloves, coriander, ginger, mint.

COOKING FRUIT

Always poach fruit; don't stew it. Drop into boiling liquid— try wine—reduce heat, and simmer until almost tender. Remove and drain immediately.

Fixes

Brown Fruit: Store cut fruit, such as apples, bananas, and pears, in a solution of 1 part lemon juice and 3 parts water. When ready to serve, rinse, pat dry, and serve.

Ripening Rock-Hard Fruits: Place in a brown paper bag. To ripen even faster, add a banana!

Nuts: Toast walnuts, pecans, and almonds in the oven at 375°F until aromatic, approximately 10 minutes.

» Toast pine nuts in a small frying pan over low heat, and stir until brown around the edges.

» Hazelnut skins are difficult to remove. So, if possible, purchase with skins already removed!

Vegetables

• •

Asparagus: Place in a pot with 1 inch of water, covered, over medium-high heat. When steam escapes, turn off, drain, and enjoy!

Artichokes: To keep artichokes from appearing brown, add lemon juice to the cooking liquid to reduce the cell breakdown. Another option is to set the artichoke hearts in a bowl of ice water with the juice of 1 lemon, and then let them sit until you are ready to use them.

Beans/Legumes/Peas:

Fresh Bean/Pea Basics

» Make sure your beans are fresh. They should snap quickly when you break them in two. Cook them in water until crisp tender.

Dried Bean/Pea Basics

» To soak beans quickly, in a large saucepan, combine dried beans, picked over, with triple their volume of cold water. Bring to a boil and cook, uncovered, over moderate heat for 2 minutes. Remove pan from heat and let stand for 1 hour. Note: Beans may break up using this method. Soak overnight if you need your beans to stay in one piece.

» Avoid tough skins by adding salt, vinegar, tomatoes, or juice after the beans are tender/cooked. Adding them too early can slow the cooking process and cause tough skins.

» If in a warm area, soak in the refrigerator to prevent fermentation.

Black Beans: Take longer to soak—soak overnight.

Lentils: Try brining them for a few hours; this will help to keep the skins intact, resulting in firmer lentils. Place 1 cup lentils and 1 teaspoon salt in a bowl. Cover with 4 cups warm water and soak for 1 hour. Drain well, then cook as normal.

Best Spices for Dried Beans: Cumin, cayenne, chili, parsley, pepper, sage, savory, and thyme.

Bean Curd/Tofu:

» Tofu, also known as Bean Curd, is made by coagulating soy bean curds and them pressing them together. It is often used as a meat substitute as it is high in protein.

» Silken tofu is made using techniques similar to yogurt making. It is best used in delicate soups, purees, or as a base for dips, dressings, and sauces. Regular tofu is made similar to cheese and can stand up to higher heat such as stir-frying.

Broccoli and Cauliflower: Cook florets that are equal in size, and be careful while steaming not to overcook. Check after 3 minutes.

Corn:

Basics

» *Make sure the kernels are firm and not shriveled. The lighter the kernel the sweeter the corn.*

» *Husking the Easy Way:* With a sharp knife, cut off the stalk end of the cob above the first row of kernels. Place 3 to 4 cobs at a time on a microwave-safe plate, and microwave on full power for 30 to 60 seconds. Then hold each ear by the uncut end. Shake the ear up and down until the cob slips free, leaving the husk and silks behind.

» *Boil*—Shuck corn and place in a large pot with enough cold water to cover. Add approximately 2 tablespoons sugar, bring to a boil, turn off the heat, and let sit for 3 to 5 minutes.

» *Grill*—Shuck and grill for 15 to 17 minutes – Don't let the grill get too hot.

» *Microwave*—Wrap shucked ear in a damp paper towel, and microwave for approximately 5 minutes. Enjoy!

Eggplant: Eggplants come in a variety of colors and sizes. Many cooks recommend slicing the eggplant, sprinkling with salt, letting it sit for 10 to 15 minutes, and then rinsing it. Generally, use salt if the eggplant needs to retain its shape, for example, with Eggplant Parmesan. If you are mashing the eggplant, you may not need to salt.

» Cooks often debate about the need to salt eggplant. For example, if you are using smaller, exotic eggplants, salting is not recommended. We recommend that you follow the recipe.

Greens You Can Cook: Remove the tough center stems, stack the leaves, and then slice thinly for consistent portions.

» **Beet Greens**—Sauté tips of beets similar to spinach.

» **Bok Choy, Napa, and Savoy Cabbage**—Great for stir-fry.

» **Cabbage: Green, Red, and Savoy**—Quick braise in butter and a braising liquid.

» **Collard Greens**—Slow braise, then cook for 30 minutes to 2 hours, depending on the recipe.

» **Dandelion Greens**—Fry bacon, remove from pan, and crumble. Set aside. Add garlic, wine, and greens to 1 tablespoon bacon fat. Sauté for 5 minutes, and then top with crumbled bacon.

» **Kale**—Fry in olive oil; slow braise until tender; or toss in olive oil and salt, and broil until crisp. Also great raw in salads!

» **Mustard Greens**—Pan steam or slow braise.

» **Spinach**—Wash and remove large stems and damaged or wilted leaves. Place in pan and sauté.

» **Swiss Chard**—Best sautéed.

» **Turnip Greens**—Slow braise or pan steam for best results.

Mushrooms—What to Use When

» **Grilling**—Cremini, Portobello, and White Button

» **Sautéing**—Black trumpet/horn of plenty, Cremini, Maitake/ hen of the woods, Morel, Oyster, Portobello, Shiitake, and White Button

» **Roasting**—Cremini, Portobello, and White Button

Wild/Fresh Morels: Always soak in lemon juice and water for about 1 hour. Little slugs like to live inside the pockets, so the lemon juice will force them to the surface for easy removal.

Don't throw away those mushroom stems: Freeze and use them for soups and stocks.

Dried Mushrooms: Dried mushrooms, such as porcini, a.k.a dried cèpes, should be large and thick in size. Avoid small, crumbly ones or mushrooms that look like they have little holes in them!

Fixes

Decaying/Old Mushrooms: These can hide nasty toxins, so if the fungi are a bit mushy or suspect, throw them out and buy fresh.

My Mushrooms Turn Dark Brown on the Sides after I Slice Them: Rub cut mushrooms with lemon juice, and they will stay a nice bright color. This does not affect the taste.

Onion Family

Onion Basics

» Always use a sharp knife to cut them. Keep the exposed cut side away from you, and run the hood fan.

» Do not cook them over high heat; they burn easily.

» Cook onions gently until translucent for a mild flavor. Sauté until golden for a strong flavor. For a sweet, carmely flavor, sauté until brown.

» Pearl Onions/Peeling—To peel pearl onions, place them in a bowl, cover with boiling water for 1 minute, and then drain and peel.

Chives—Generally, use only the finely chopped leaves. Chive flavor will intensify dramatically overnight, so beware. Chive flowers can be used for soups or as a pretty addition to a salad; they are edible!

Garlic—Place clove with skin onto a cutting board and use the flat handle of a large knife. Smash clove to easily remove the skin. Or microwave with the skin on clove for 15 seconds; the skin will peel right off!

» Never let it brown, cook very gently, and add toward the end of a sauté.

Leeks—Clean them very well, and generally only use the white part; the green tends to be stringy.

Shallots—Shallots are very delicate; do not brown them—sauté gently.

STORE ONIONS IN A COOL DARK
PLACE FOR UP TO 3 MONTHS.

Peppers, Sweet—For the most part, sweet peppers (red, orange, yellow, and green) are interchangeable in recipes.

Summer Squash—Examples include zucchini and yellow squash. Must be firm and heavy with a thin skin. If rind is tough or skin is black, don't bring it home.

Winter Squash—Examples include acorn and butternut squash. Must be heavy with a hard shell. If the squash has black, watery spots, it's best to avoid it!

Vegetables Tips

» *Vegetables for a Puree*: Potatoes, carrots, white turnips, cauliflower, broccoli, spinach, green peas, cooked lentils, chickpeas, beans, parsnips, celery root, and rutabagas. Try some of the above for baby food too. Just mix with a bit of cooking liquid and, voilà, homemade baby food!

» *Vegetables for Par Boiling or Blanching*: Turnips, cauliflower, brussels sprouts, green beans, and broccoli are great for a quick parboil or blanch.

» *Soup Suggestions:* If you're making a stew or soup, first add vegetables like potatoes, onions, thickly sliced carrots, green peppers, and corn. Add mushrooms, turnips, cauliflower, brussels sprouts, green beans, or broccoli in the last 15 minutes. Enjoy.

Starches

. . . .

Couscous: Check to see if you are using instant or traditional couscous. If it is instant, follow the instructions. If you have traditional roughly ground, hard durum wheat, cook it similar to rice: add couscous to the pan, cover with water, and bring to boil. Let couscous simmer for 20 minutes, uncovered. Fluff with a fork and enjoy!

Pasta: Never add oil to pasta when it is cooking. Oils will prevent sauce from sticking to pasta. Don't rinse your pasta. Rinsing will wash off the good starches that give pasta its flavor.

» Cooking on a Hot Day? Or Are Your Burners Full? Try soaking your pasta noodles for 90 minutes in 4 quarts of water plus 1 teaspoon salt per pound of pasta. Then add to your favorite baked dish like ziti or lasagna.

Polenta: Check to see if you have instant or traditional milled cornmeal/ polenta. Traditional can take up to 40 minutes, and it requires constant stirring, while instant is much faster!

» Some chefs suggest cooking polenta overnight in a slow cooker on low.

» Try polenta boiled with a bit of butter. Or, once boiled, fry it in butter.

Potatoes—**What to Use When**

» ***Baking/Roasting***—Russet,
Burbank, Idaho, Yukon Gold,
round red, and fingerling

» ***Boiled***—New potatoes, round
red, Yukon Gold, russets, white potatoes, and fingerling

» ***Fried***—Russets and Yukon Gold (For super crispy fries, try frying potatoes twice: once at 325°F and again at 375°F.)

» ***Mashed***—Yukon Gold and white potatoes

Poke potatoes with a fork before cooking and to test for doneness.
When checking for doneness, the fork should come out easily. If
not, the potatoes need more time.

Best Spices for White and Red Potatoes: Basil, chervil, chives,
coriander, dill, marjoram, oregano, paprika, parsley, rosemary, tarragon, thyme. We recommend adding only one.

Fix

Gummy Potatoes? Don't use an electric mixer or food
processor to mash potatoes; they will become too gluey!

» Add butter before dairy in mashed potatoes. Milk
first = gummy potatoes.

Sweet Potatoes vs. Yams: Sweet potatoes and yams are two very different tubers. Sweet potatoes are yellow or orange in color. Yams have brown or black skin. Yams are also higher in sugar content.

» Microwave for 4 to 8 minutes. Pierce with a fork to make sure they are done.

» Wrap the tubers in aluminum foil, pierce the foil to vent, and/ or place tubers directly onto foil or a cookie sheet, as they tend to drip while cooking. Cook both varieties at 350°F for approximately 1½ hours. Pierce with a fork to see if properly cooked— the fork should remove easily.

Best Spices for Sweet Potatoes: Nutmeg, cinnamon, and allspice.

Rice

White Rice:

» Arborio is Italian rice used in risotto and paella. It cooks creamier than other varieties.

» Basmati is grown in India, aged, and aromatic. We recommend long grain for regular use. Rinse imported rice such as basmati. Many people rinse all rice, saying it improves the flavor and helps to make it less gummy—you decide.

Brown Rice: A true rice whose bran layer has not been polished off. Presoaking brown rice can cut down on cooking time. Place rice and room temperature water into pot (1½ cups water per 1 cup of rice) and let soak for 6 to 24 hours. Cook for 30 minutes or per recipe.

Wild Rice: Wild rice takes twice as long to cook as white rice and requires 3 times the amount of water.

Alternatives: Foods such as quinoa, amaranth, and chia are not actually grains like rice. They are pseudocereals and not related to the grass family. They can, however, be used and cooked similar to grains such as rice.

Fix

Grains Too Wet? Drain grains in a colander and place over low heat for a minute or two. Be careful not to burn the grains!

Substitute chicken or beef broth for water to yield a richer flavor when cooking all grains, pastas, and potatoes.

Sauce 101

Thickening Basics:

» Dissolve 1 teaspoon of starch into 1 tablespoon of cold liquid, preferably the same liquid used to make the sauce (e.g. wine, stock, milk, or water) to make a slurry. When it comes time to thicken your sauce, add a few tablespoons of hot sauce to the slurry to slowly warm it, and then incorporate the slurry into the entire sauce. Stir constantly until thickened.

» Heavy cream will require less flour than stock to reach the same consistency.

» Add cold butter to pan sauces. Cold butter resists separation. Margarine is not butter, and it will not taste or cook up the same as butter.

Soups	1 tablespoon flour to 1 cup liquid
Cream sauces	2 tablespoons flour to 1 cup liquid
Soufflé bases	3 tablespoons flour to 1 cup liquid

Other Thickeners:

Arrowroot—Ideal when you want a clear or transparent sauce, as arrowroot is more transparent than cornstarch. Arrowroot is easily digestible as well, but beware it can thicken suddenly! Best used at the end of cooking just before serving.

Buerre Manié—This uncooked roux is perfect if you have a sauce that didn't quite thicken. Use 1 part softened butter with 2 parts flour. Form mixture into balls the size of large peas. Add a few balls at a time to warm sauce or pan juices while whisking.

Cornstarch—A great last minute thickener for oriental foods. Do not use cornstarch when high temperature and extended cooking time are required.

Egg Yolk—Add 2 or 3 yolks to 1 cup liquid or 2 yolks to 3 table-spoons crème fraîche. Stir yolks to break them up, and then gradually add a small amount of hot liquid, stirring constantly until yolks are warmed/tempered. Return egg mixture, slowly, to the hot liquid in the pan, and stir over low heat. Make just before serving, and watch carefully to prevent curdling.

Pureed Vegetables—Vegetables used in preparing soups, sauces, or a mirepoix cooked with a roast. Can be strained and pureed then used to thicken soups or sauces.

Fixes

Oh No, It's Curdled…Remove the sauce from the heat and whisk in an ice cube. Or try whisking 1 egg yolk and 1 tablespoon water in a small saucepan over low heat until creamy. Remove egg mixture from the heat, and gradually whisk curdled sauce drop by drop into creamy egg yolk mixture. If the sauce curdled badly, you may need to start over.

» *Hollandaise sauce:* If it starts to curdle while you are adding the hot butter, pour 1 tablespoon hot water into the sauce while whisking.

» *Béarnaise sauce:* If you are cooking béarnaise on a humid day, use clarified butter to keep the sauce from breaking apart.

» *Quiche Custard That's Curdled:* If you are cooking a quiche that includes onions or leeks, add a bit of cornstarch. The cornstarch interferes with the proteins in the onion mixture and helps create smooth custard for your quiche.

Sauce Remedies

» *Lumpy:* If the sauce is lumpy, force it through a fine sieve to remove the lumps, return to pan, and heat gently while whisking constantly.

» **Salty:** Add an acid like vinegar; lemon or lime juice; canned, unsalted tomatoes; sugar; honey; or maple syrup. If a soup or stew is too salty, throw in a peeled potato for about 15 to 20 minutes then remove. For cream or butter sauces, add more cream.

» **Spicy:** Add a fat like butter, cream, sour cream, cheese, or olive oil. Or add a sweetener like sugar, honey, or maple syrup.

» **Sweet:** Add an acid or seasonings like vinegar or citrus juice. Or add seasonings like chopped fresh herbs or a dash of cayenne. Or try adding a pinch of espresso powder.

» **Thin:** Cook the sauce on low for another 15 to 30 minutes longer. It should evaporate and become more concentrated. If the sauce starts to scorch, pour it into a clean pan, leaving behind the scorched bits, and keep going. Or add beurre manié to thicken.

Tips about Butter and Oils

· ·

Butter

Wait for the butter to stop foaming before sautéing. This shows the cook that the pan is hot enough to properly sauté.

» Use cold not softened butter for pastry. Good pastry depends on distinct pieces of cold butter.

» Slip butter under the skin of any poultry. It bastes the meat while it cooks.

» To measure solid butter, fill a measuring cup with 6 oz. water, and then add butter until it reaches 8 oz. This will give you 4 tablespoons of butter.

Oils

Olive Oil—We recommend the first press extra virgin; anything lower in grade will affect flavor. Keep in mind that most of the flavor of olive oil gets lost when you are  cooking with it, so save the really good stuff for cold applications such as salads, dips, or dishes already cooked, such as pasta. Use the lesser grades for cooking.

Peanut Oil—Use primarily for deep frying, as it cooks better at higher temperatures. Interchangeable with cottonseed oil.

Sesame Oil—This oil has a strong, distinct nutty flavor, and is used in Asian cooking.

Vegetable Oil—Oils such as corn or canola have subtle flavors, which can affect some foods. Corn and canola oils are interchangeable with each other.

Oil-Based "Vegetable Shortening"—Contains corn or soybean oil that has been refined, hydrogenated, and deodorized. Best used for frying and baking.

How to Handle Your Spices

. . . .

Chilies

Fresh Chilies/Hot Peppers:

» The volatile oils in the flesh and seeds of chilies and peppers can make your eyes water and your hands sting! Wearing rubber gloves is the best precaution.

» Rinse chilies in cold water, and remove the stems. Partially split each chili and brush out the seeds, as well as the veins, with your fingers. Removing the veins can also reduce the hotness of the chilies.

» The heat of fresh chilies is from the delicate membrane attaching the seeds to the chili. If you like it hot, leave the membrane and seeds intact. For a more delicate flavor, remove both then cut into strips.

Dried Chilies: Tear these into small pieces; again, we suggest wearing gloves. Cover with boiling water for 10 minutes or up to 1 hour. If you desire a smokier flavor, do not soak the chili, but char or blacken the dried chilies over a medium-high heat until darkened and somewhat softened. The water from the steam will soften the chili.

Herb Basics

Check for freshness by crumbling a small amount between your fingers, then take a whiff. If it releases a lively aroma, it's fresh. If it doesn't, it's best to get a new jar!

Stems: Should I Use Them in My Recipe? Parsley and cilantro—yes, use them; they are wonderful when finely chopped. Thyme, rosemary, mint, oregano, tarragon, and sage—no, their stems are either too woody or are simply unusable.

Drying Herbs Fast: For sage, rosemary, thyme, oregano, basil, mint, and marjoram leaves, place fresh, clean leaves, stems removed, in a single layer between two paper towels on the microwave turntable. Cook for 30 seconds. Check. If not dry, use fresh paper towels, and microwave another 30 seconds until dry.

Need a Stronger Herb Flavor? Try Blooming Your Herbs: To intensify the flavor of dried herbs, sauté them for a minute or two in butter and/or oil before adding any liquid. Add the remaining items, and continue with the recipe!

Spice Grinders—Cleaning: Place several tablespoons of raw white rice into the grinder, and pulverize to a fine powder. The rice will absorb residual spice particles and oils. Discard the rice, and enjoy your clean grinder.

Cheese Basics

. . . .

> DO NOT REMOVE THE RIND FROM
> SOFT, RIPE CHEESES.
> DO REMOVE THE RIND FROM HARD
> OR WAXED RIND CHEESES.

Types of Cheeses

Soft/Mild Flavor—Chevre/goat cheese (can be mild or strong depending on the variety), cottage cheese (mild with curds), cream cheese/Neuchatel (very mild flavor), ricotta (similar to cottage cheese).

Soft Cheese/Strong Flavor—Liederkranz (similar to Limburger) and Limburger (mild flavor but very pungent odor!).

Crumbly—Feta (salty, tangy taste).

Semi-Soft/Mild Flavor—Monterey, mozzarella, Muenster, provolone.

Hard/Sharp Nutty Flavors—Asiago, cheddar, Parmigiano-Reggiano, Parmesan, Romano.

Semi-Hard/Mild—Edam, Gruyère (a type of Swiss cheese), Swiss, Gouda, fontina.

Mold Ripened—Blue, Gorgonzola, Roquefort, Stilton.

Mold Ripened/Soft Flavor—Brie, Camembert. Smell the cheese to check for ripeness. If it has an ammonia odor, it is overripe. Also, check the firmness. It should not be terribly soft but only somewhat firm.

Ask your cheese counter attendant for more diverse varieties!

What to Do with It Now?

» Store cheese in a fresh wrapper after each use, preferably aluminum foil. It will stay fresh longer and not mold.

» Keep cheese at a consistent temperature, ideally between 50°F and 55°F. In most refrigerators, the best place for cheese is the vegetable compartment.

» The longer the cheese has aged, the more full-bodied the flavor. Translated, you'll use less in cooking.

» Shred, grate, or break cheese into small cubes to use in cooking. This allows for even melting, and the dish won't be stringy.

Meats

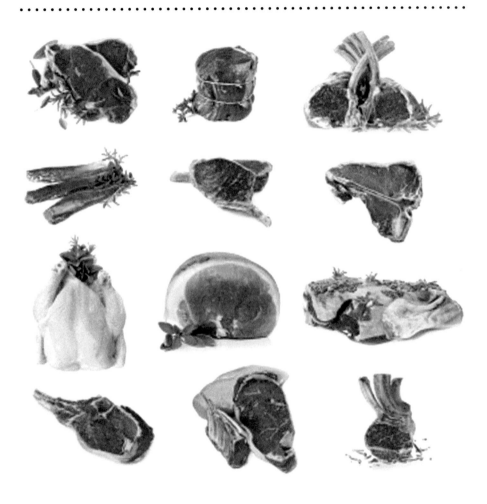

Best Advice—Invest in a good meat thermometer. It will save you time and possibly your dinner too!
• Be sure to check the "Use before date" and freeze no longer than 6 months!

Basics

» Always use coarse salt and freshly ground pepper when seasoning your beef. The larger grains distribute more evenly

» Use wood chips to enhance the flavor when grilling meat. Bank
   coals on one side of the grill, or if gas with three burners, you
   may try grilling at medium, off, medium flame. Use vents to
   regulate heat.

» Season with pepper after searing for a solid pepper taste.
   Season before searing for a milder pepper bite.

Cooking

Roasting—Fast and High Temp: Tenderloin, top sirloin roast, rack
of lamb

» 5 pound roast – Preheat the oven to 450°F. When you put your
   meat into the oven, turn the temperature down to 350°F. Cook
   18-20 minutes per pound for medium rare.

Roasting—Slow and Low Temp: Rib toast—first cut, boneless
blade roast, center rib roast, leg of lamb, center loin roast, country
style ribs, rib chops, spareribs, ham, pork butt, and pork shoulder.

*Grilling—*Great for all cuts, just check your recipe for time/temp
variables.

> *Save your juices for pan gravy*
> *Beef—add red wine.*
> *Pork—add orange or berry jam.*

> *Take meat off the heat when the thermometer*
> *reads 5°F below desired doneness. Tent with*
> *foil and let it rest for at least 5 minutes. This*
> *will allow the juices to flow, and the meat will*
> *continue to cook to desired doneness.*

Meat Cooking Guidelines

Chefs vary in their opinions as to when a piece of meat is done. Here are two guidelines—you can choose what is best for you and your family.

Cook time will vary based on meat thickness.

Guide #1

	Beef	Pork	Lamb
Rare	125°F	NA	125°F
Medium Rare	130°F		130°F
Medium	135°F	150°F	140°F
Well Done	160°F	160°F	160°F

(Ground meats such as beef, pork, and poultry should be cooked to 160°F.)

Guide #2

The **National Restaurant Association** recommends the following **minimum** internal temperatures:

	Beef	Pork	Lamb
Steaks		145°F for 15 seconds	
Roasts		145°F for 4 minutes	
Ground Meat/all types		155°F for 15 seconds	

Beef by Definition

> GRADING IS DETERMINED BY THE US DEPARTMENT OF AGRICULTURE AND THE US BEEF INDUSTRY. GENERALLY, AS THE GRADE DECREASES SO DOES THE MARBLING, TENDERNESS, AND JUICINESS OF THE BEEF.

Prime: Highest quality grade may include cattle fed specific diets. Prime meats have the highest fat content and will generally have a good amount of marbling. Examples include Black Angus and Kobe.

US Choice: These meats have less marbling than prime but still have good quality. Formally known as "Select."

US Standard: Lower grade beef with less marbling.

US Utility, Cutter, Canner: Primarily used by food processors or canners.

Fixes

{ *Round, boneless steaks, such as tenderloin and rib eye, hold better if tied. Veal and lamb shanks also benefit from tying to keep the meat attached to the bone for extra flavor.* }

Roasts Falling Apart? To Tie or Not to Tie:
Tying meat keeps it compact and helps with even cooking. All-natural cotton or linen twine is best, as it won't taint the meat or burn in the oven.

» *Tying a Butcher's Knot:* You can make this knot without a spare finger to hold the string in place. Begin by tying an overhand knot as if tying a bow, but loop the free end around the other end once more, and then pull the ends to tighten the twine around the meat.

» *Tying Beef Tenderloin:* Tenderloins are generally narrow at one end. The thinner end must be tucked under itself and tied so that it will cook at the same time as the rest of the meat. Tuck the thin end portion, about the last 6 inches, underneath the tenderloin, and secure with 12-inch length of twine. Tie off the rest of the roast at 1½-inch intervals. Tie the twine firmly but not too tightly; you don't want to squeeze out all of the juices.

» *Tying a Standing Rib Roast:* If left untied, the outer layer of meat on a standing rib roast tends to separate from the rib eye muscle as it cooks, making for an unattractive dish. Note: Tie a piece of twine around both ends of the roast, running the twine between the bones.

CROWN PORK ROAST OR PRIME RIB
ASK YOU BUTCHER FOR A C&C: CUT AND CRADLE. HE WILL CUT THE BONE OFF AND TIE IT BACK TO THE MEAT. WHEN DONE COOKING, SIMPLY REMOVE THE BONE AND ENJOY!

PORK ROASTS AND CHOPS ARE ALWAYS BETTER WHEN BRINED BEFORE COOKING!
PORK RIBS ARE BETTER PRECOOKED IN A SLOW 250°F OVEN FOR 2 TO 3 HOURS BEFORE GRILLING.
SEE CHAPTER THREE FOR RECIPES!

Poultry

· ·

USDA ORGANIC LABELS ARE GOVERNMENT REGULATED. LABELS SUCH AS HUMANE CERTIFIED, ALL NATURAL, RAISED WITHOUT ANTIBIOTIC, AND VEGETARIAN FED, ARE NOT STRICT GUARANTEES OF COMPLIANCE.

REFRIGERATE ALL POULTRY FOR NO LONGER THAN 2 DAYS AND FREEZE FOR UP TO 9 MONTHS. USE IMMEDIATELY UPON THAWING!

Poultry Basics

» Always handle your poultry with care.

» Keep your poultry cutting board separate from your other boards.

» Make sure that the raw poultry does not touch other food items.

» Wash your hands and utensils after handling raw poultry.

» Cook poultry thoroughly.

How Much Do I Need? Plan on 1 pound per serving when buying a bird that is 12 pounds or less and ¾ pound per serving if the bird is more than 12 pounds. If you are serving poultry pieces plan on two pieces per person.

Cooking Guidelines: Cover the poultry with foil, and insert your thermometer probe directly through the foil and into the deepest part of the breast. Keep the bird covered until the final temperature is achieved.

» Cook all poultry to a minimum internal termperature of 165°F

» Don't open the door to baste the bird; open doors let heat out and lengthen the cooking time.

» Let the bird rest at least 30 minutes before you carve. This will allow time for the juices to reabsorb into the bird.

» Loosen the skin and work butter, seasoned as you please, under the skin of the bird (for recipe see Chapter Three: Home Made).

Not Stuffing the Bird? Season the cavity with salt and pepper (do not season the cavity if you have brined the bird). Add 2 peeled and quartered onions, 2 carrots, 2 celery stalks, 2 bay leaves, and a few sprigs of parsley and thyme. When the bird is cooked, simply remove and discard the veggies.

Chicken By Defintion

Broiler	1½ to 2½ pounds
Fryer	3 to 3½ pounds
Poaching chicken	3 to 3½ pounds
Roaster	4 to 7 pounds

Turkey: What Is It, and Where Do I Begin?

Fresh Turkeys: These turkeys have never been stored at a temperature below 26°F. They should be refrigerated and cooked within 2 days of purchase.

Frozen Turkeys: These turkeys have been flash frozen to a temperature of 0°F or below. The quality of the meat does not suffer. Many frozen turkeys have been labeled as self-basting or basted, which means that they have been injected with oil, juices, and seasonings.

» To thaw a turkey, transfer it from the freezer to the refrigerator and wait. A 20 pounder will take 4 days to thaw—a 16 pounder about 3 days. A thawed turkey will keep in the refrigerator for 2 days before cooking.

» Thaw early! The above are only guidelines. It can take a bit longer for the bigger birds.

Natural Turkey: These turkeys have been minimally processed and contain no artificial ingredients or colors.

Free-Range or Free-Roaming Turkeys: These birds have eaten only organic feed (no antibiotics or growth hormones).

Heritage Turkeys: Same idea as heirloom tomatoes. These birds are raised by small boutique farmers. Generally, they are old-fashioned breeds, such as Bourbon Red or Jersey Buff. Check the Internet for sites, as generally these are mail order only.

Best Spices for Poultry: Allspice, basil, bay, cinnamon, curry, dill, fennel, garlic, ginger, lemongrass, mustard, paprika, rosemary, saffron, sage, savory, tarragon, and thyme.

Fixes

Brining—Brining will make your meats moister! To put it in technical terms, the salt in brine unravels the proteins around the sheath that makes up the muscle tissues, allowing more water to enter. These unraveled proteins in the sheath contract far less as they cook, allowing for moister meats.

We recommend that you brine poultry. This extra step will be worth the effort.

» If brining, always rinse off the brine and allow to dry prior to cooking (for recipe, see Chapter Three: Home Made).

» If you plan to brine overnight, halve the salt by ½ cup per gallon of water.

Poultry	Water	Salt	Timing
4 (6 to 8 oz.) boneless breasts	2 qt.	¼ cup	30 min to 1 hour
4 pounds bone-in pieces	2 qt.	½ cup	30 min to 1 hour
Whole bird (3 to 4 pound)	2 qt.	½ cup	30 min to 1 hour
Whole bird (6 to 8 pound)	2 qt.	½ cup	1 hour
Whole bird (over 8 pounds)	See Home Made section for recipe–soak for 8–12 hours.		

Note: Make sure the bird is covered with the brine!
Kosher and enhanced poultry may be presalted and may contain excess salt. *Do not* brine these varieties!

Brine ducks per above recipe. Store-bought ducks generally weigh 3 to 5 lbs. Allow 11/2 lb. per serving.

> **DON'T FEEL LIKE BRINING?**
> **SALTING ALTERNATIVE**
> USE KOSHER SALT; TABLE SALT WILL MAKE THE BIRDS TOO SALTY!
> ONE TEASPOON PER POUND–RUB ALL OVER INSIDE AND OUTSIDE OF BIRD, AND THEN STORE IN THE REFRIGERATOR UP TO 24 HOURS.

Shellfish and Seafood

. . . .

Shellfish

Mussels and Clams: Only purchase if the shells are completely closed. If they are open it means the shells are old or have been poorly handled. Cook in broth until the shells open. Discard those shells that do not open.

Scallops:

» Sea scallops are ivory or lightly colored. White sea scallops have been processed, usually not as fresh

» Bay scallops are smaller than sea scallops. They are usually much sweeter than sea scallops as well.

Lobster and Crabs: Make sure they are alive when you purchase them. Follow recipe for cooking times.

Oysters: Generally appear in 5 sizes. Each area of harvest implants a unique flavor.

Shrimp and Prawns: Should be fresh, dry and firm. Ask if they have been previously frozen. If they have been frozen then do not re-freeze! Use immediately.

Seafood

Seafood Basics: First, the store should smell right. It should smell like the sea, not like stinky, sour fish!

Check for the following:

» Smooth, shiny skin with scales well adhered to the flesh

» Consistent, elastic, and firm flesh

» Tight belly, not too swollen or faded

» Lucid convex eyes

» Rosy, moist gills

» Tail and dorsal fins intact

» A pleasant smelling fish with a mild scent of the sea

» Fish can be purchased frozen, but beware of fish with freezer burn.

» Fish is irregular in shape just by its nature. Tuck the tail under the fillet for more even cooking

> *Soak fresh fish in milk for 20 minutes or up to 1 hour. This will take away any leftover fishy smell!*

> *If you're not using the fish right away, put it in a storage bag, cover it with ice packs, and store it in the back of the refrigerator. Or fill a Ziplock bag with water, add fish, and freeze!*

How to Cook it

Sautéing—Best for thin fillets, such as sole or flounder.

» Pat the fish dry and season with salt. Let fish stand about 5 minutes.

» Place 1 cup flour on a plate and dredge the fish through the flour. At this point, you can simply sauté, or you can dredge again in egg (2 eggs beaten) and then in bread crumbs. We prefer a mix of bread crumbs or crackers and finely grated parmesan cheese.

» Melt 1 tablespoon olive oil and 1 tablespoon butter over high heat. When butter melts, reduce to medium high, add fish, and cook until golden. For thicker fillets, it may be necessary to finish the fish in a 425°F oven for 5 to 10 minutes or until done.

Grilling—superheating the grill will prevent sticking.

» Place a disposable aluminum pan upside down over grill. Cover for 5 minutes to superheat the grill and help prevent sticking.

» Scrape grate clean with grill brush, then wipe it with oil-dipped paper towels. Place fish on grill, perpendicular to grates.

» Grill fish until browned—2 to 3 minutes (if fish has skin, place skin-side up). Slide a spatula underneath fillet to lift and flip over. Continue cooking until desired doneness.

Pan Searing

» Heat vegetable oil over high heat until smoking. Don't use olive oil; it will burn!

» Add fish and cook for 30 seconds.

» Reduce heat to medium high, and cook fish until browned. Flip and continue until done.

Braising—The key is a tight-fitting lid.

» Over medium-high heat, sauté 1 sliced onion, 4 cloves garlic, and 2 tablespoons olive oil until onion is soft. Add ½ cup white wine and 14 oz. can diced tomatoes.

» Nestle fish, seasoned with salt and pepper, into sauce, and spoon sauce over fish. Cover, reduce heat to medium low, and cook until desired doneness.

Poaching

» Bring 6 cups water, 1 cup white wine, juice of 1 lemon, 1 teaspoon salt, ½ coarsely chopped onion, and 1 coarsely chopped carrot to a simmer. Add a few whole peppercorns, a bay leaf, and a few sprigs of fresh parsley or thyme. Simmer for 20 minutes. Reduce to low then add fish. Cover and poach to desired doneness—6 to 10 minutes.

Best Spices for Fish: Basil, bay, cayenne, celery seed, chives, curry, dill, fennel, garlic, ginger, lemon peel, mustard, oregano, parsley, rosemary, thyme, saffron, sage, savory, tarragon, and marjoram.

Temperature Guidelines

Salmon	125°F
Tuna	110°F
All other fish	140°F, or until flakes easily with a fork.

Desserts: from Chocolate to Meringue

· ·

Chocolate by Definition—Basics for All Chocolate Used in Baking

Chocolate Liquor: A dark, thick liquid made by grinding the nibs extracted from dried, fermented, roasted cacao beans. This process melts the cocoa butter, creating the liquor. It is pure, unsweetened, and the base ingredient for all other processed chocolates.

» About 55 percent of chocolate liquor is cocoa butter, a natural fat responsible for giving chocolate its unique texture.

Cocoa Powder: Chocolate liquor fed through a press to remove all but 10 to 24 percent of the cocoa butter. To counter the harsh, acidic flavor of natural cocoa, the powder is sometimes treated with an alkaline solution such as baking soda—often called "Dutched." Dutched powder is darker than traditional powder and has a slightly different flavor.

Beware—there are no advisable substitutions for cocoa, as chocolates have too much fat to take the place of cocoa.

» Cocoa powder contributes a lot of chocolate flavor with little additional fat, making it wonderful for hot beverages, cakes, cookies, or recipes that already contain a lot of butter.

» For a stronger, deeper chocolate flavor, try "blooming" cocoa powder in hot liquid, such as water or coffee. This dissolves the remaining cocoa butter and disperses water-soluble flavor compounds.

Sweet Chocolate (dark chocolate): Must contain 15 percent chocolate liquor and often more than 60 percent sugar.

Semisweet: Combination of chocolate liquor (at least 35 percent) and cocoa butter.

Unsweetened or Bittersweet: Pure chocolate liquor that has been cooled and molded into bars. Suspended in the cocoa butter are particles of ground cocoa solids that carry the chocolate flavor.

Milk Chocolate: Contains 10 percent chocolate liquor and 12 percent milk solids.

» Generally weak chocolate flavor and not used in cooking.

White Chocolate: Technically not chocolate because it contains no cocoa solids. However, it does contain at least 20 percent cocoa butter.

White Chocolate Chips: These may contain palm oil in addition to (or instead of) cocoa butter. Generally, brands with the most fat are desirable.

Melting Chocolate/Tempering

Caution...Do not burn or scorch chocolate; it will affect flavor. And be sure to break the chocolate into smaller pieces for easier/faster melt times.

Options:

» *Double Boiler:* This is the preferred method for melting all types of chocolate, avoiding both scorching and the formation of steam droplets. Simply place chocolate blocks or chocolate chips in the top of a double boiler over hot, not boiling, water.

» **Direct Heat:** Because chocolate scorches so easily, we don't recommend this method. There are three musts: very low heat, a heavy saucepan, and constant stirring.

» **Microwave Oven:** Unwrap, break blocks in half, and place desired amount in microwave-proof measuring cup or bowl. Microwave at high (100 percent) for half the minimum time listed below. Stir. Continue to microwave until chocolate is softened. Stir. Allow to stand several minutes to finish melting. Stir again. If unmelted chocolate remains, return to microwave and heat for an additional 30 seconds. Stir until fluid.

1 block (1 oz.)	1½ minutes
2 blocks (2 oz.)	1½ to 2 minutes
3 blocks (3 oz.)	2 to 2½ minutes
4 blocks (4 oz.)	2½ to 3 minutes

Note that in a microwave oven, chocolate blocks and chips will keep their shape even when they are softened. Stir to determine whether chocolate is fluid and melted.

Stiff or Grainy Chocolate? Usually caused by a wet utensil or steam droplets. Simply stir in 1 teaspoon solid vegetable shortening (not butter) for every 2 oz. of chocolate.

» Stir the melting chocolate periodically with a wire whisk to help blend and discourage scorching.

Is It Any Good/Is It Still Fresh? Break a bar; the sharp snap should produce only even textured fissures, with no splinters or crumbs. The fragrance should be deep and heady. Taste it; it should melt smoothly on your tongue, with a rich, nutty, and lightly acidic flavor. And finally, dusty looking chocolate is still OK if it meets the above requirements.

» Note: It's a good idea to keep chocolate (well wrapped, of course) in a cool place during prolonged periods of heat and high humidity.

Gray Color? Temperatures above 78°F will cause chocolate to melt. The cocoa butter then rises to the surface and forms a grayish discoloration called "cocoa butter bloom." This is OK!

» Milk or semisweet chocolate kept in the refrigerator may obtain condensation. This condensation may cause the sugar to dissolve and rise to the surface as "sugar bloom." Neither bloom affects the quality or flavor of chocolate. Once melted, the chocolate will regain its original color.

Baking Basics

BASICS
- Double-check your measurements, especially with shortening or lard. Just because the package says it contains ½ cup, it may not be exact—best to measure or use a scale.
- Save calories and do not butter your parchment while baking. It's OK; it will not stick.
- Use a bay leaf in your flour to keep out weevils and other little buggers.

» **Silicone Muffin Tins** can be flexible and rubbery. They don't allow the items to brown well and are awkward to get into the oven!

» **Aluminum Baking Pans** may react with the acids in tomato-based recipes.

» **Light Colored Tinned or Stainless Steel Cake Pans** may brown and release poorly.

» **Dark Finishes, Lightweight Cookie Sheets** warp easily, and sheets with only one handle or four sides make it hard to slide off finished cookies.

» **Ceramic and Disposable Aluminum Pie Plates** can be flimsy and affect browning.

» **Loaf Pans without Handles and Light-Colored Pans** can deter browning.

» **Glass or ceramic pans** lower the oven temperature by 25°F.

It is best to use light-colored cookie sheets to ensure even browning for cookies or cakes and to use parchment paper to line pans for easy clean up—works great for cookies too.

Cakes:

» Use a toothpick to test for doneness; however, it's OK if the pick has a few stray crumbs on it! As long as there is not a lot of raw dough attached, the cake should be moist and perfect.

» Try using cocoa instead of flour for the pan coating. It adds a bit more flavor!

» Use cake flour if the recipe calls for it. Using all-purpose flour will yield a cake that is more compact with a heavier structure.

If you are cooking two pans in one oven, stagger the pans and rotate halfway through cooking for even cooking.

For buttercream frosting, try using half butter and half vegetable shortening for a light, fluffy frosting.

Fixes

Is Your Batter Too Thin? If the batter is too thin, let it rest for 20 or 30 minutes. This works for muffins too!

Is the Cake Overdone/Dry? Cut the ends off, cut into squares, and serve with chocolate sauce or fruit.

Is the Cake Flat? Try stirring in the flour by hand instead of using the mixer. This will allow larger air pockets to form.

Cookies:

» Almost all cookies can be frozen in their dough form. Simply portion out cookies on a cookie sheet and freeze until hard. Move frozen dough to separate bags for later baking!

» Roll dough between two pieces of parchment for even baking, and don't reroll more than once; otherwise, the cookies will be too dry.

» Do not use wax paper for cookies; the wax that is exposed will melt!

» If the recipe directs you to chill the dough, do so! It is important for consistency while baking.

Pies:

» Roll the dough out immediately after you take it out of the refrigerator. Warm dough will tear and stick! If dough is sticking, add more flour to your work surface as you roll it out.

» Filled pastry crusts do not freeze well. However, unfilled crusts freeze great.

» Marble makes an ideal rolling surface because it retains the cold.

» Chill the pie shells until firm before baking.

» An 8- or 9-inch pie will use one 1 pound 5 oz. can of pie filling; a 10-inch pie will need two cans.

Fixes

Need a Flakier Crust? Use a ratio of ½ vodka and ½ ice water in your recipe.

Pie Filling Boiling Over? Cut seams in the top of fruit pies to prevent them from boiling over.

Burnt Crust Edges? To prevent crust from over-browning, cover the outer rim with foil, and then remove it during the last 15 minutes of baking.

Avoid a Soggy Crust. Partially bake pastry crust in 425°F oven for 14 to 16 minutes (line crust with foil topped with dried beans or pastry marbles). Brush with egg yolk, and then return to oven for 2 more minutes. Fill crust with filling and finish recipe!

Meringue: A dessert or pie topping made with whipped egg whites and sugar.

» Separate eggs directly from the refrigerator; they will break cleanly, and the yolks of cold eggs are less likely to shatter.

» It is critical that no yolk enter the mix. Even a slight bit will prevent the whites from reaching full volume.

» Egg whites that have been stored in the refrigerator for up to 2 weeks produce a better meringue than fresh ones.

» You can make your own superfine sugar by whirling granulated sugar in the blender or food processor

» Beware of making meringue on a humid day. It will weep and not look attractive. Additionally, you cannot freeze meringue.

Baking Tips

Hard Brown Sugar? Place the hardened brown sugar in a bowl with a slice of bread. Cover with plastic wrap and microwave for 10 to 20 seconds. No bread handy? Use an apple slice instead. Another hint: put the sugar in a pie plate and heat at 225°F for 3 to 4 minutes.

» Store brown sugar with a terra cotta Brown Sugar Bear. Give it a brief soak in water before placing it with sugar into a sealed plastic bag/container. You can find these bears online or at a specialty cooking supply store.

» *Caramel*: Making homemade caramel is difficult. Save yourself time and frustration and purchase what you need.

» *Crystallized Honey*: Open a glass honey jar, put it in a saucepan filled with 1 inch of water, and heat until it reaches 160°F.

» *Currents and Raisins*: Soak them in rum or Madeira for 1 hour, drain, and use in cooking. Drain the liquid to drink with your sweet treats.

CHAPTER TWO

Substitutes

WHAT TO DO WHEN YOU DON'T HAVE IT!

Baking Powder
Bread Crumbs
Chocolate
Eggs
Flour
Lemons
Milk/Creams
Mushrooms
Onion
Spices
Sugars
Syrups
Thickeners

Have you ever started cooking and suddenly realized that you don't have all of the ingredients? Well, take a look at some handy substitutes to help you cook quickly and effectively!

First, there's no substitute for accuracy. Read the recipe carefully, but when you've done that and you're still missing some things...

Baking Powder: One teaspoon = ½ teaspoon cream of tartar plus ¼ teaspoon baking soda plus ¼ teaspoon cornstarch.

Bread Crumbs: One cup = 1 cups cracker crumbs or Panko. Note: texture may be altered! For a fine texture, blitz in a food processor until desired consistency.

Butter: One cup = 1 cup vegetable shortening by volume, and 16 oz. or 1 lb. of butter = approximately 14 oz. vegetable shortening by weight. You can substitute margarine, as well, but it will affect the flavor.

Chocolate: *Warning, Warning!* These substitutes ignore the many important differences between butter, oil, and cocoa butter. For example, a pan of fudgy brownies made with cocoa powder and butter instead of chocolate baking squares will usually turn out cake-like and dry.

Unsweetened Chocolate: One square (1 oz.) = 3 tablespoons unsweetened cocoa powder plus 1 tablespoon shortening or canola oil or 1 oz. envelope premelted, unsweetened chocolate product.

Semisweet Chocolate: One oz. semisweet chocolate pieces = 3 tablespoons unsweetened cocoa powder plus 3 tablespoons sugar and 1 tablespoon butter.

Sweet Baking Chocolate: One bar/4 oz. = 3 tablespoons cocoa plus 4½ tablespoons sugar plus 2⅔ tablespoons shortening or butter.

Cocoa Powder: Do not substitute! Recipes ask for cocoa powder for its fat content or lack thereof. So, in this case, we recommend going out to the market!

Chocolate: One oz. = 3 tablespoons carob powder plus 2 tablespoons water.

Eggs

One whole egg = 2½ tablespoons dry sifted eggs beaten with 2½ tablespoons water.

One egg white = 1 tablespoon dried egg white plus 2 tablespoons water or 2 tablespoons frozen egg whites thawed.

Flours

All-Purpose Flour: One cup = 1⅛ cup cake flour, 1¼ cups rye flour, 1 cup spelt flour, ⅝ cups potato flour, or 1 cup minus 2 tablespoons rice flour.

Note that you can also substitute barley flour, buckwheat flour, and whole-wheat flour for all-purpose flour. Again, you may note a slight taste difference.

Cake Flour: One cup = 1 cup less 2 tablespoons all-purpose flour, sifted.

Pastry Flour: One cup = ¾ cup all-purpose flour plus ¼ cup cake flour.

Self-Rising Flour: One cup all-purpose flour plus 1¼ teaspoons double-acting baking powder and ½ teaspoon salt.

Lardoons: If you cannot find salt pork, use bacon or pancetta.

Lemons
. . . .

Lemon Juice: One teaspoon = ½ teaspoon vinegar.

Lemon Rind: One teaspoon = ½ teaspoon lemon extract.

Milk/Creams
. . . .

Whole Milk: One cup = ½ cup evaporated milk plus ½ cup water, 1 cup water plus ⅓ cup nonfat dry milk powder plus 2½ teaspoons butter, ¾ cup half-and-half and ¼ cup water, or ¾ cup 2 percent milk and ¼ cup half and half.

Soy or Almond Milk: One cup = 1 cup skim milk plus 2¼ teaspoons cream

Soy, almond, rice, and hemp milk can be used interchangeably; however, you will note a slight taste difference. Also, these milks are similar to skim milk in consistency and are not recommended as a substitute for whole milk, heavy cream, or half-and-half.

Buttermilk: One cup = 1 tablespoon lemon juice or vinegar plus enough milk to make 1 cup (let stand 5 minutes) or 1 cup plain yogurt

Crème Fraîche: See Chapter Three: Home Made

Coffee Cream (20% Butterfat): One cup = 3 tablespoons butter plus ⅞ cup of milk.

Light Cream: One cup = 1 tablespoon melted butter plus enough milk to make 1 cup.

Half and Half: One cup = 1½ tablespoons butter plus ⅞ cup of milk, ½ coffee cream and ½ milk, or ⅔ skim milk and ⅓ cup heavy cream.

Heavy Cream: One cup = ¾ cup milk plus ⅓ cup melted butter (this will not whip). Do not substitute whipping cream; the fat content is different and may alter your recipe.

Sour Cream: One cup dairy = 1 cup yogurt or ⅓ cup butter and ¾ cup buttermilk. Nonfat or low-fat yogurt may not taste or act the same as full-fat yogurts in this substitution. Tip: Add off heat or at very low heat only.

Low-Fat Sour Cream: Two cups low-fat cottage cheese and 3 tablespoons fresh lemon juice. Process in a blender until smooth.

Whipping Cream: One cup—oh the options (see recipes in Chapter Three: Home Made)

Clotted Cream: No substitute. The method used in England is very time consuming and includes raw milk direct from the cow, which is difficult, if not impossible, to find in the United States.

Mushrooms: Six oz. canned = ½ lb. fresh.
Dried 3 oz. = 1 lb. fresh

Onion: One small onion = 1 teaspoon onion powder; 1 table-spoon dried, minced onion; or 3 to 4 shallots.

Sugars

A word of caution: Substituting sugars usually alters the texture a bit, and you may notice a slight taste difference. That said, when in a pinch...

Brown Sugar is granulated sugar with some molasses mixed in.

» Process 1 tablespoon molasses into 1 cup of granulated sugar.

» Dark brown sugar: Use 2 tablespoons molasses into 1 cup of granulated sugar.

Confectioners' Sugar/Powdered Sugar = granulated sugar that has been pulverized in a food processor into a powder.

» Process 1 cup of granulated sugar plus 1 teaspoon cornstarch in a blender or spice grinder for 3 minutes then sieve.

Maple Sugar: One tablespoon = 1 tablespoon granulated sugar.

Non-Caloric Sweeteners: One-quarter teaspoon = 1 teaspoon granulated sugar (obviously, it will now have calories).

Raw Cane Sugar: Granulated sugar, or if you can find it, turbinado or demerara are close substitutes. Turbinado is raw sugar that has been "cleaned." You can try to use the above brown sugar recipe, but it won't taste exactly the same. Demerara is the British version of turbinado.

Sugar/Granulated: One cup = 1 cup brown sugar packed or 2 cups sifted powdered sugar.

Superfine Sugar: This has a fine texture, which makes it dissolve faster in liquids (it's more common in the United Kingdom).

» Process 1 cup plus 2 teaspoons of granulated sugar in a food processor for 15 to 30 seconds.

Syrups
. . . .

Molasses: One cup = 1 cup honey or ¾ cup granulated sugar.

Honey: One cup = 1¼ cups sugar plus ¼ cup water.

Maple Syrup: One cup = ½ cup maple sugar or 3 parts honey to 1 part water.

Corn Syrup: One cup = ½ cup granulated sugar and reduce the liquid in the recipe by ¼ cup.

Thickeners
. . . .

Cornstarch: One tablespoon = 2 tablespoons flour. Best if boiled to create thickening action.

Arrowroot: One and a half teaspoons = 1 tablespoon flour. Two teaspoons = 1 tablespoon cornstarch. Best used for fruit sauces and desserts. Arrowroot should not be boiled to thicken.

Flour: One tablespoon = 1½ teaspoons cornstarch, potato starch, rice starch, arrowroot, or 2 teaspoons quick-cooking tapioca.

Egg Yolks: Two yolks = 1 whole egg. Use 2 yolks per cup of liquid, and always add yolks to a small amount of the hot liquid slowly. Then mix with entire sauce to keep the eggs from cooking overly fast.

Tomatoes

. . . .

Tomatoes: One cup packed or canned = ½ cup tomato sauce plus ½ cup water plus a dash of salt and sugar or ¼ cup tomato paste plus ¾ cup water.

Tomato Paste: Use ketchup.

Tomato Juice: One cup = ½ cup tomato sauce plus ½ cup water plus a dash of salt and sugar.

Tomato Soup: One cup sauce plus ¼ cup water.

Tomato Sauce: One cup = ¾ cup tomato paste plus ¼ cup water.

Vanilla: One Bean = 1 teaspoon vanilla extract.

Wines/Liquors

. . . .

Liquor: One-half cup liquor (rum, bourbon, or whiskey) = ¼ cup unsweetened fruit juice or broth.

Wine: One-half cup wine = ½ cup apple or white grape juice (for white wine) or ½ cup unsweetened grape juice (for red wine).

» Port, brandy, vermouth, or red wine can be used interchangeably, but a slight flavor difference may be noted.

Dry Yeast: One package active dry yeast = 1 cake of compressed yeast.

Seasonings

SALT

Table salt, kosher salt, fleur de sel and others are easily interchangeable if you base your measurements on weight.

1 teaspoon table salt = 1 heaping teaspoon kosher salt

¼ table salt = ¼ cup plus 1 tablespoon kosher salt

Kosher salt is not recommended for baking as it does not dissolve easily.

Herbs: ½ to 1 teaspoon dried = 1 tablespoon fresh.

Allspice: One teaspoon = ½ teaspoon cinnamon plus ⅛ teaspoon ground cloves.

Garlic: One clove = ⅛ teaspoon garlic powder.

Ginger: One-half teaspoon ground = 2 teaspoons grated fresh gingerroot, or 1 tablespoon gingerroot = ⅛ teaspoon powder.

Horseradish: One tablespoon fresh = 2 tablespoons bottled.

Mustard: One tablespoon prepared mustard = ½ teaspoon dry mustard plus 2 teaspoons vinegar.

CHAPTER THREE

· ·

Home Made

FROM APPLE PIE SPICE TO VANILLA AND EVERYTHING IN BETWEEN

Apple Pie Spice:

½ teaspoon cinnamon   ⅛ teaspoon allspice

¼ teaspoon nutmeg   ⅛ teaspoon cardamom

Bouquet Garni:

3 to 4 sprigs parsley   1 medium bay leaf

¼ teaspoon dried thyme   2 to 3 sprigs celery leaves

Barbeque Rub:

¼ cup brown sugar   ¼ cup sugar

2 tablespoons garlic salt   1 tablespoon onion salt

1½ teaspoons celery salt   ¼ sweet paprika

1 tablespoon chili powder   1 tablespoon black pepper

1½ teaspoon sage   ½ teaspoon allspice

¼ teaspoon cayenne   ⅛ cup salt

Pinch of cloves

Basic Brine: One cup of kosher salt for each gallon of water. You can add white or brown sugar, honey, fruit juice, cider, beer, and/or wine for additional flavoring, as well as peppercorns, garlic, and fresh herbs. Ice and keep cold.

Poultry: In a large stockpot, add ½ gallon tap water, ⅔ cup sugar, and 1 pound of salt (weigh your salt, as weight changes depending on the type of salt). Bring to a boil, cook until salt is dissolved, remove from heat, and cool completely. Place bird in a large storage container/cooler, add 2 quarts vegetable broth, and fill with ice or very cold water to cover. Set in cool place and flip after 4 hours. Brine for 8 to 12 hours. Note: keep brine at 40°F, check periodically, and add ice packs or sealed bags of ice to maintain the temperature

Pork: Three quarts water, ½ cup kosher salt, ¼ cup whole peppercorns, and ¼ cup sugar. Bring to a boil, remove from heat, and cool. Brine pork for 3 hours or overnight. You can also add 2 teaspoons garlic, 1 teaspoon thyme, and 2 bay leaves depending on your tastes. Another idea is to substitute beef or chicken broth for some or all of the water.

Dry: In a large skillet, place 3 tablespoons black peppercorns, 2 teaspoons white peppercorns, 2 teaspoons coriander seeds, and 6 bay leaves. Fry until fragrant, let cool, and then crush. Add ½ cup kosher salt and 2 tablespoons light brown sugar. Rub on a 12 to 14 pound turkey, and let sit for 6 to 7 hours. Rinse off and bake. (See Chapter One: Meats, Poultry, and Seafood for more brining ideas.)

Clarified Butter: Cut 8 oz. (2 sticks) unsalted butter into small pieces and place in a small saucepan. Melt over medium heat then skim off the foam. Slowly pour off clear, yellow liquid, leaving behind the residue of milk. Stays fresh in the refrigerator for 2 to 3 weeks and can be frozen.

» Great for searing food at higher temperatures without burning.

Buttermilk: One cup of milk and 1 tablespoon of either vinegar or lemon juice. Let set for 5 minutes. If you have heavy cream, you can also place 1 cup of heavy cream in a sealed container and shake vigorously for about 5 minutes until you start to see the cream turn into butter. Voilà, buttermilk!

Cheese/Mascarpone:

1 (8 oz.) package of cream cheese   1/3 cup sour cream
¼ cup whipping cream
Beat well.

Cheese/Yogurt: Wrap plain yogurt, low fat is best, in a double layer of cheesecloth, and suspend a few inches over the bottom of a jar; cover and refrigerate for 12 hours. Cheese will keep for 3 or 4 days. Great on toast, mixed with herbs as a dip, on a baked potato, or as a spread for sandwiches.

Crème Fraîche: Heat 1 cup of heavy cream (not ultrapasteurized) to 85°F. Transfer cream to a jar with a tight-fitting lid, and add 1 tablespoon buttermilk. Shake the mixture, covered tightly, for at least 1 minute. Let stand at room temperature at least 8 hours. Keeps chilled for 4 to 6 weeks.

Creole Seasoning:

3 teaspoons paprika	2 teaspoons salt
2 teaspoons garlic powder	1 teaspoon black pepper
1½ teaspoons onion powder	1 teaspoon cayenne pepper
1 teaspoon dried oregano	1 teaspoon dried thyme

Coconut Milk: One cup diced, fresh, or shredded coconut plus 1 cup scalded milk. Add together in blender or food processor and mix until smooth. Pour through two layers of cheesecloth. Refrigerate. Better for curries and stir-fry sauces—not ideal for baking.

Fish Sauce: One tablespoon soy sauce blended with 1 finely minced anchovy fillet.

Fine Herbs: Use for scrambled eggs, omelets, fish, chicken, mayonnaise, butters, and sauces. For best results add the mixture at the last minute. Can be made with fresh or dried herbs depending on what you feel like.

Dried	Fresh
1 teaspoon thyme	¼ cup chervil
1 teaspoon basil	¼ cup chives
1 teaspoon savory	¼ cup parsley
1 teaspoon grated lemon peel	¼ cup tarragon
1 teaspoon marjoram	Finely mince all of the above together.
1 teaspoon sage	

5 Spice Powder: Equal parts star anise, fennel seed, peppercorns, whole cloves, and cinnamon. Put in spice grinder and grind.

Ganache: Use as a glossy, glaze-like frosting and rich filling for cakes and chocolate truffles. The quantities of ingredients depend on how you use the ganache. Ganache can be refrigerated for 1 week or frozen for 3 months. Before using, let stand at room temperature to soften or melt over warm water.

Frosting/Filling: Chop 1½ pounds bittersweet chocolate into small pieces, and place in a dry metal bowl. Scald 2½ cups heavy cream, and pour over chocolate. Let stand a few minutes, and then stir gently until mixture is smooth.

» For filling, refrigerate the mixture until it's chilled but not firm, and then whip it until it lightens in color and becomes stiff enough to spread; use it right away.

Glaze: Mix similar to frosting recipe. Let the mixture cool slightly to room temperature, and then pour over the top of the cake.

Truffles: Twelve oz. of bittersweet chocolate, chopped finely. Add ½ cup scalded heavy cream. Stir 2 tablespoons of Armagnac, brandy, or orange liqueur into the mixture until smooth. Chill until firm (this will take several hours, and you may want to prepare the ganache a day in advance and refrigerate it overnight). Scoop the mixture with a melon baller, and roll the balls in sifted cocoa. Refrigerate at least ½ hour before serving.

Garlic Oil: Separate and peel the skin from whole garlic cloves. Put them in a jar, and fill it with any kind of vinegar you have (as long as it has at least 5 percent acidity) until the cloves are covered. Allow the cloves to soak for 24 hours, drain. If you notice the cloves have discolored, that is OK; it will not affect the taste. Put the cloves in a clean jar, and cover them with oil—olive oil if possible. Store in the refrigerator for up to 5 months, and you can use the garlic as you would fresh garlic and the oil as flavored oil! Note: the oil will solidify in the refrigerator, but the taste is fantastic and the oil will melt once at room temperature.

Garlic/Roasted: Cut entire bulb in half; do not skin. Drizzle both sides with olive oil, and wrap in aluminum foil. Roast at 350°F for 20 minutes.

Ghee: Common in Indian and Middle Eastern cooking. Place 1 pound of butter in medium saucepan over medium-high heat. Bring butter to boil. Once boiling, reduce heat to medium. The butter will form foam that will disappear. Ghee is done when a second foam forms on top of butter, and the butter turns golden in approximately 7 to 8 minutes. Brown milk solids will be in the bottom of the pan. Gently pour the butter through a fine mesh strainer or cheesecloth into a heat-proof container. Store in an airtight container. Ghee does not need refrigeration and will keep in an airtight container for up to 1 month.

Garam Masala:

1 tablespoon cardamom seeds	1 teaspoon whole cloves
1 teaspoon black peppercorns	1 teaspoon black cumin seed
2-inch stick of cinnamon	1/3 whole nutmeg
Curl of mace	

Grind in a coffee grinder or spice mill until you have fine powder.

Gremolata: Generally used for topping lasagna or braises. You can also add rosemary, chives, or sage depending on the dish.

Zest of 1 large lemon	1 large clove of garlic, minced
2 tablespoons minced parsley	2 teaspoons olive oil
½ teaspoons salt	¼ teaspoons pepper

Mix it all together, and sprinkle as you see fit!

Harissa: Serve with stews, salads, brochettes, and couscous, or use as a meat marinade. Use different dried peppers to adjust the heat factor to your tastes. Depending on your time, place peppers in a dry cast iron pan, blacken, and then soak in water to increase the smoky flavoring.

10 to 12 dried red chili peppers	3 cloves garlic
½ teaspoons salt	2 tablespoons olive oil
1 teaspoons ground coriander	1 teaspoons ground caraway seeds
½ teaspoons cumin	

Soak chilies in hot water for 30 minutes or until very soft. Combine chilies, garlic, salt, and olive oil in a blender, and mix. Add remaining ingredients, and mix into a paste. Drizzle with olive oil, and store in the refrigerator for 1 month.

Herbes de Provence: Use for meat, fish, or poultry.

One tablespoons of each of the following: savory, rosemary, thyme, oregano, basil, marjoram, and fennel seeds.

Mirepoix/Soffritto

French: An equal amount of carrots, celery, and onions cut finely, cooked in butter or olive oil. Use for stocks, stews, and soups.

White Mirepoix: Leeks, mushrooms, onions, parsnips, and celery. Use for stocks, stews, and soups.

Italian Mirepoix/Soffritto—Also Called Sofrito in Spanish: An equal amount of onions, garlic, and celery. Use red or white onion instead of the more traditional yellow.

Mirin: Two tablespoons white wine or sake plus 1 teaspoon sugar.

Mulled Wine Spice: One cinnamon stick and 1 teaspoon cardamom pods, crushed to small pieces.

2 teaspoons orange peel	2 teaspoons lemon peel
2 teaspoons cloves	2 teaspoons crystallized ginger
1 teaspoon black peppercorns	

Tie together in a bag, or place in a tea steeper.

Olive Oil/Infused: Simmer your selection of dried herbs in 2 cups extra virgin olive oil for 5 minutes; do not fry. Let cool. Place in a clean container, adding a few of the simmered herbs to your liking. Store oil in the refrigerator for up to 1 month.

Peanut Butter: Two tablespoons olive oil plus ¼ cup shelled peanuts. Blend in a mixer until finely ground.

Pinzimonio: Served in Italy in small dishes as a dip for raw vegetables, such as celery, fennel, radishes, and carrots.

2 tablespoons olive oil   2 tablespoons balsamic vinegar
Salt/pepper

Poultry Seasoning:

1 tablespoon rosemary   1 tablespoon oregano
1 tablespoon ground ginger   1 tablespoon marjoram
1 tablespoon thyme   1 teaspoon sage
1 teaspoon pepper

Pumpkin Pie Spice:

½ teaspoon cinnamon   ¼ teaspoon ginger
⅛ teaspoon allspice   ⅛ teaspoon nutmeg

Quatre Épices: Use for charcuterie and dishes that cook for a long time like stews.

2 tablespoons white peppercorns   ¼ teaspoon freshly grated nutmeg
½ teaspoon (about 12) whole cloves   ¼ teaspoon ground cinnamon
¼ teaspoon ground ginger
Place all in a spice grinder and grind.

Sugar

> **Colored:** Place ½ cup granulated sugar in a bowl. Add about 5 drops of food coloring, and mix thoroughly. Push sugar though a fine mesh sieve, and then spread on a pie plate to dry.

> **Vanilla:** After using a fresh vanilla bean for a different dish, rinse the bean and let it dry completely. Then add to a canister of sugar. Use after 2 to 3 days in coffee or whipped cream.

Homemade Vanilla: Two vanilla beans per 1 cup of vodka. Scrape the beans into the vodka, drop the bean pod in, and store in a dark, cool place for 1 month. Shake the bottle every couple of weeks. Strain through a coffee filter.

Whipping Cream: Here are several different ways to make Whipping Cream:

» Three-fourths cup whole milk, heated gently with 4 oz. (1 stick) unsalted butter until butter melts. Pour into a blender, not a food processor, and whip for 4 to 5 minutes. Store in the refrigerator for at least 24 hours. Whip as you would whip cream.

» Two-thirds cup well-chilled evaporated milk, whipped.

» One cup nonfat dry milk whipped with 1 cup ice water.

» One can evaporated milk plus 3 tablespoons lemon juice.

» One-half cup nonfat dry milk dissolved in ⅓ cup cold water. Whip to soft peaks, and then add 1 tablespoon lemon juice. Whip then add 2 to 4 tablespoons sugar. Whip until stiff peaks.

CHAPTER FOUR

Location, Location, Location

STORAGE AND SHELF LIFE

WHERE IN YOUR CABINET AND HOW LONG WILL IT LAST?

STORAGE AND SHELF LIFE

Keep meat in the bottom portion of the refrigerator. Here is a guide from the National Restaurant Association ServeSafe Course Book as well as the 2009 FDA Food Code Guidelines regarding how to store your food in your refrigerator.

Keep your foods in the refrigerator in this order from top to bottom.

Ready-to-Eat Foods—Salads, Vegetables, Fruits
Whole Fish
Whole Meat
Ground Meat
Poultry

If salads, vegetables, fruit and ready-to-eat foods are kept in a sealed/closed drawer under other items, it is OK in your home refrigerator. Simply check to make sure that juices from the fresh fish, meats, and poultry cannot penetrate the drawers. That is where cross contamination can begin.

Apples: Refrigerate for up to 3 or 4 weeks.

Baking Powder and Baking Soda: Keeps in the pantry for up to 6 months.

Blackberries: Refrigerate uncovered in a single layer for up to 4 days. Do not rinse until you are ready to use them.

Blueberries: Refrigerate loosely covered for 1 or 2 weeks. Do not rinse until you are ready to use them.

» Freezing berries—Place cleaned berries in a single layer on a cookie sheet. Place in freezer for 15 to 30 minutes. Remove and put in freezer bags.

Butter: Keep in the refrigerator, but you can freeze both salted and unsalted. In the refrigerator, butter can keep for up to 1 month after the sell by date.

Bread: Store it in the freezer to keep it fresh.

Cheese: Some cheeses freeze better than others do, but wrap them all tightly in plastic then freeze those listed below:

» Cream cheese dip—When made with heavy cream.

» Cheddar, brick, Swiss. Freeze in pieces of ½ pound or less.

» Camembert, Port du Salut, mozzarella, Liederkranz, provolone, Parmesan, Romano, Brie

» Blue cheese—Becomes a bit more crumbly but great for salads or salad dressings.

» Baked cheese—Freeze your cheese rounds before baking them; the cheese will keep its shape better.

Note: Don't freeze cream cheese! It will become dry and crumbly on the inside and moist on the outside.

Cherries: Place in a colander in the refrigerator. With stems they will last about a week; without stems they will last 4 to 5 days. Hard to freeze.

Chilies: Store sliced in a brine solution of 1 tablespoon salt per cup of water in a sealed container in the refrigerator for up to 3 weeks. Wash off brine and use as normal.

Chocolate: Chocolate products will stay fresh for well over a year if stored in a cool, dry place (65°F to 70°F). Unsweetened dark chocolate can last 2 years. It's best to keep an eye on temperature and humidity. Try not to store chocolate in the refrigerator, as the cocoa butter can easily absorb flavors from other foods.

Coffee: Opened beans stored in an airtight container should be used within 10 to 12 days. If you are storing longer, some chefs suggest storing in the freezer; others suggest a cool, dark place, such as the refrigerator. You decide what location is best for your beans.

Cranberries: Purchase them when they are in season, and freeze for up to 6 months.

Flour: All-Purpose—Store in the pantry for 1 year.

Flour: Stone ground and natural grains—Best stored in the refrigerator, if possible, for up to 8 months.

Flour: Whole wheat and cornmeal—Should be placed in sealed bags and stored in the freezer for up to 2 years.

Grains: Barley, polenta, bulgur, wheat—Buy only what you need. They can be stored in the pantry for up to 1 year. Beware these items are very susceptible to moths.

Lemons/Limes: Cut them up, and store them in the freezer for up to 4 months. Use as needed.

Mushrooms: Store loose mushrooms in a Ziploc bag, and leave the bag slightly open. Or leave them in their original container. If you only use a partial container, wrap the top with plastic wrap and return to the refrigerator. Don't store mushrooms in paper bags, and don't cover them with damp paper towels. This only speeds up the deterioration. Mushrooms stay fresh for up to 3 days in the refrigerator.

Olive Oil: Store opened for 3 months and unopened for 1 year. Keep in the pantry along with canola, corn, peanut, and vegetable oils.

» **Want to Keep Exotic Oils Fresh Longer?** Keep them in the refrigerator. Bring them to room temperature before using, and enjoy! Great for sesame and walnut oils.

» **Infused Oils**: If you are using fresh herbs for the oil, store in the refrigerator for 1 week. If you are using dried herbs, it can keep for up to 1 month in the refrigerator. Note: we recommend dried herbs, as fresh herbs can contain more water and aid in contamination of the oil.

Peaches: Store on the counter, as the cold air in the refrigerator can damage their flesh. Store on the counter for 1 to 3 days.

Potatoes: Keep in a paper bag, away from onions, in a cool, dry place. Most should last for several months; however, thinner-skinned varieties will keep about 1 month. They can also be stored in the refrigerator but may not last as long.

» Store fresh potatoes even longer. Fill a large jar with water and fill with peeled, cut-up potatoes. Cover and keep in the refrigerator for several weeks. Hint: Use the leftover water as a soup base!

Spices—Fresh:

» Basil and Coriander/Cilantro—Store roots in fresh water just like a bouquet! (You can also mash the cilantro roots with fresh garlic and salt for a more intense flavor, and then add to sauces.)

» Ginger root—Slice in dime size pieces and freeze.

Spices Dried: One year (whole—2 years).

Sugars—Granulated, Honey, and Molasses: Long lasting.

Syrups—Maple: Two years unopened, 1 year opened.

Tea: Best stored in the pantry. Storing in the freezer or refrigerator may cause condensation, which will affect the taste/quality of the tea. Store for up to 18 months.

Tomatoes: Don't refrigerate! Keep fresh tomatoes on the counter, unwashed, with the stem side down. If you must freeze extras, core and freeze them whole in freezer bags. Freezing preserves flavor better than canning. Hard, unripe tomatoes? Store them in a paper bag with a banana or apple.

Vanilla: Long lasting. Even after 10 years, it can still be good!

Vinegars: Long lasting.

Yeast—Instant or Active Dry: Four months in the freezer.

CHAPTER FIVE

Equivalents/ Conversions

MEASUREMENTS

How Much in a Can, How Much in a Cup
Food Equivalents: Pounds to Cups and Back Again…
Oven Temperature Conversions

To be sure of your weights/measurements, it's best to purchase a good scale. It's worth the investment!

> *The plumpest grain of wheat originally determined weight. So, in some cookbooks you will still see weight measured in grains!*

MEASUREMENTS

Liquid and Dry by Volume

STANDARD MEASUREMENT		METRIC
0.034 oz.		1 ml
	1000 ml	1 L
1/8 teaspoon	dash	
1 teaspoon		5 ml
3 teaspoons	1 tablespoon	15 ml
1 tablespoon	½ oz.	15 ml
1 oz.	2 tablespoons	29 ml
⅛ cup	1 oz./2 tablespoons	29 ml
¼ cup	2 oz./4 tablespoons	60 ml
⅓ cup	5 tablespoons + 1 teaspoon	78 ml
⅜ cup	6 tablespoons	88 ml
½ cup	4 oz./8 tablespoons	118 ml
⅝ cup	10 tablespoons	147 ml
⅔ cup	10 tablespoons + 2 teaspoons	158 ml
¾ cup	6 oz./12 tablespoons	180 ml
⅞ cup	14 tablespoons	207 ml
1 cup	8 oz./16 tablespoons	236 ml
1 pint	16 oz./2 cups	500 ml
1 quart	32 oz./4 cups/2 pints	946 ml
4.23 cups		1000 ml/1 L
1 gallon	4 quarts/16 cups	3.78 L

Dry Weight

0.35 oz.		1 gram/15.43 grains
2.21 lb.		1 kilogram/1000 grams
1 oz.	1/16 lb.	28.35 grams/16 drams
4 oz.	¼ lb.	120 grams
8 oz.	½ lb.	225 grams
16 oz.	1 lb.	454 grams

THE FOLLOWING DRY MEASUREMENTS ARE FOR RAW FRUITS AND VEGETABLES

1 pint = 1/16 peck	1 quart = ⅛ peck
1 peck = 8 quarts or ¼ bushel	1 bushel = 4 pecks
1 liter = 18 pints	

How Much in a Can, How Much in a Cup

IN A CAN?

8 oz. can = 1 cup

10½ oz. can = 1¼ cups

12 oz. can = 1½ cups

1 lb. can = 1¾ cups

16 to 17 oz. can = 2 cups

IN YOUR CUPBOARD...
Baking powder: 2 teaspoons = 1 oz.
Butter: 2 teaspoons = 1 oz.
Butter: 2 cups = 1 lb.
Flour: 4 cups = 1 lb.
Flour: ¼ cup = 240 grams
Rice: 1 cup = 240 grams
Salt, fine: 4 teaspoons = 1 oz.
Salt: 1 tablespoon = 35 grams/1 cup = 140 grams
Sugar, granluated: 1 teaspoon = 15 grams
Sugar, granulated: 2 tablespoon = 1 oz.
Sugar, granulated: 2 cups = 1 lb.
Sugar, powdered: 2½ cups = 1 lb.

Drinks
1 DASH = 6 DROPS
3 TEASPOONS = ½ OZ.
1 PONY = 1 OZ.
1 JIGGER = 1½ OZ.
1 LARGE JIGGER = 2 OZ.
1 STANDARD WHISKEY
GLASS = 2 OZ.
1 PINT = 16 FLUID OZ.
1 FIFTH = 25.6 FLUID OZ.
1 LITER = 33.92 FLUID OZ.

Food Equivalents: Pounds to Cups and Back Again

· ·

Apples, fresh: 1 lb. = 3 cups pared and sliced

     Dried: 1 lb. dried = 3½ lbs. fresh

Apricots, dried: 1 lb. = 3¼ cups

     Fresh: 1 lb. = 3 cups cooked

Bananas: 3 medium = about 1¾ cups mashed

Baking powder: 1 cup = 5½ oz.

Beans:

     Green beans, fresh: 1 lb. = 2½ cups cooked

     Kidney beans, dried: 1 lb. = 2½ cups = 6 cups cooked

     Lima beans, dried: 1 lb. = 2½ cups = 6 cups cooked

     Navy beans, dried: 1 lb. = 2 cups = 5 cups cooked

Butter: 4 oz. Stick = 8 tablespoons = ½ cup

     Whipped: 1 lb. = 3 cups

Bread crumbs: ¼ cup dry = 1 slice dried bread; ½ cup soft = 1 slice soft bread

Cabbage: 1 lb. head = 4½ cups shredded

Carrots, fresh, no tops: 1 lb. = 3 cups shredded or 2½ cups diced

Cheese, shredded or crumbled: ¼ lb. = 1 cup

     Cottage cheese: ½ lb. = 1 cup

     Cream cheese: 3 oz. = 6 tablespoons

Bulk cheese: 2 oz. yields ½ cup grated; 4 oz. bulk = 1 cup grated

Chocolate, baking bits: 11.5 oz. = 2 cups

Clams: 1 qt. unshucked = 1 serving of 6 to 8 medium shucked per person

     8 qt. unshucked = 1 quart shucked

Cocoa: 1 lb. = 4 cups ground

Coconut: 1 lb. = 4 cups shredded

Coffee: 1 lb. = 5 cups ground = 40 to 50, 6 oz. cups

Cookies, chocolate wafer: 27 cookies = 1½ cup crushed

       Vanilla wafer: 38 cookies = 1½ crushed

       Cornmeal: 1 lb. = 3 cups

       1 cup uncooked = 4 to 4½ cups cooked

Cornstarch: 1 lb. = 3 cups

Couscous: 1 cup dry = 2½ cups cooked

Crabmeat: 1 lb. = 2 cups

Crackers, graham: 21 squares = 1½ cups crushed

       Saltine: 29 squares = 1 cup crushed

Cream, whipping: 1 cup unwhipped = 2 to 2½ cups whipped

Dates: 1 lb. unpitted = 2½ cups pitted

Eggs:

       5 to 6 whole = 1 cup

       12 to 14 yolks = 1 cup

       8 to 10 whites = 1 cup

Eggplant: 1 medium = 1 lb.

Fish: 1 lb. = 1 serving. Fillets, boned and cleaned: 1 lb. = 3 servings

Flour, all-purpose: 1 lb. = 4 cups

Gelatin: ¼ oz. envelope = about 1 tablespoon

Lemons, medium size:

       Juice of 1 = 1 to 3 tablespoons

       1 rind, grated = 1 to 1½ teaspoon

Lime: Juice of 1 = 1 to 2 tablespoons

Lentils: 1 lb. = 2¼ cups = 5 cups cooked

Lobster: ½ large (2 lb. plus) = 1 serving

Marshmallows: 20 large = 3 cups miniature

Meat: 1 lb. = 2 cups ground

Mushrooms, fresh: 8 oz. = 3 cups sliced = 1 cup cooked

       Dried: 3 oz. = 1 cup rehydrated

Mussels: 3 qt. = 4 servings

Nuts:

      Almonds, whole shelled: 3½ lb. = 1 lb. shelled

      Whole, shelled: 1 lb. = 2 cups whole, chopped and finely chopped

      Slivered: 4 oz. = 1 cup

      Hazelnuts/filberts: 1 lb. unshelled = 3¼ cups

      Peanuts: 1½ lb. unshelled = 3 cups shelled

      Pecans: 2½ lb. unshelled = 1 lb. shelled

      Walnuts: 5½ in shell = 1 lb. shelled = 3½ cups

Oats:

      Oatmeal: 1 cup uncooked = 1¾ cups cooked

      Oats, steel cut: 1 cup uncooked = 4 cups cooked

      Oats, rolled: 1 cup uncooked = 1⅓ cups cooked

Food shapes, sizes, and cooking methods vary; therefore, equivalent may not mean exact!

Olives: 24 large = 1 cup sliced

Onions: 1 medium = approximately ½ cups chopped

Oranges: 1 medium = 6 to 8 tablespoons juice and 2 to 3 tablespoons rind

Oysters: 1 qt. drained and shucked = 6 servings

Pasta, uncooked: 1 lb. = 5 cups or 6 to 8 servings Macaroni: 1 cup uncooked = 2 to 2¼ cups cooked

> Egg noodles: 1 cup uncooked = 1½ cups cooked

> Spaghetti: 1 lb. = 6½ cups cooked

Peaches/Pears: 4 medium = 2 cups sliced

Peas, split: 2¼ cups = 5 cups cooked

Peppers: 1 large = 1 cup diced

Pomegranate: 1 average = ½ cup pulpy seeds

Poultry, 12 lb. or less: 1 pound per person

> 12 lb. or more: ¾ lb. per person

Potatoes, raw: 1 lb. sliced = 3½ to 4 cups

> 3 medium sized cups = 2¼ cups cooked or 1¾ cups mashed

Plums: 1 lb. raw = 2 cups cooked

Prunes: 1 lb. pitted and dried = 2¼ cups chopped

Radishes: 1 bunch = about 1 cup

Raisins: 1 lb. = 2¾ cups

Rhubarb: 1 lb. fresh = 2 cups cooked. (Leaves can be poisonous if cooked, so watch out!)

Rice, white uncooked: 1 cups = 2 cups cooked

      Rice, wild uncooked: 1 cup = 3 to 3½ cooked

      Rice, brown uncooked: 1 cup = 3 to 3½ cooked

Scallops, bay: 1 lb. = 4 servings

Shrimp, depending on size: 2½ lb. in shell = 1 lb. shelled, about 4 servings

Strawberries: 1 quart = 4 cups sliced

Sugar:

      1 lb. granulated = 2 cups

      1 lb. brown = 2¼ cup (packed firm)

      1 lb. confectioners = 3½ cups (sifted)

      1 lb. powdered = 21/3 cups

Tapioca: 4 tablespoons pearl = ½ to 2 tablespoons quick cooking

Tea: 1 lb. = 120 cups

Tomatoes: 1 lb. = 2 cups pureed

Wheat germ: 12 oz. = 3 cups

Yeast, compressed: 1 cake, ⅗ oz. = 1 package active dry yeast

Oven Temperature Conversions

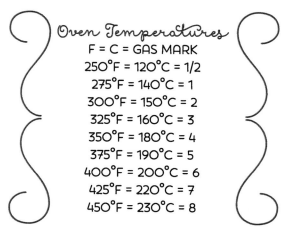

Oven Temperatures

F = C = GAS MARK
250°F = 120°C = 1/2
275°F = 140°C = 1
300°F = 150°C = 2
325°F = 160°C = 3
350°F = 180°C = 4
375°F = 190°C = 5
400°F = 200°C = 6
425°F = 220°C = 7
450°F = 230°C = 8

Celsius/Centigrade to Fahrenheit
Multiply by 9, divide by 5, and add 32.

Fahrenheit to Celsius/Centigrade
Subtract 32, multiply by 5, and divide by 9.

I.E., 212°F – 32 = 180 x 5 = 900/9 = 100°C

CHAPTER SIX

Entertaining

TABLE SETTING GUIDELINES
Quantites to Serve Twenty-Five

TABLE SETTING GUIDELINES

When setting a formal table, it is always best to go with the correct table setting guide—see below:

Quick Tips

1 BOTTLE OF WINE = 6 GENEROUS SERVINGS
1 8-GALLON BEER KEG = 85 12-OZ. SERVINGS
2 GALLONS JUICE/ICED TEA = 32 8-OZ. SERVINGS
1 POUND COFFEE = ABOUT 65 6-OZ. SERVINGS

1 16-OZ. PACKAGE POTATO CHIPS = 16 HANDFULS
1 12-OZ. PACKAGE PRETZELS = 12 HANDFULS
PLAN 1 OZ. NUTS PER PERSON

WHAT TO PUT ON A CHEESE BOARD

BRIE
CHEVRE/GOAT CHEESE
CAMEMBERT
CHEDDAR
EDAM
GOUDA
MONTEREY JACK
MUNSTER
STILTON
SWISS
PROVIDE A DIFFERENT SPREADING
KNIFE FOR EACH CHEESE!

QUANTITIES TO SERVE TWENTY FIVE

(double or triple depending on your party.)

• •

Baked beans	1 gallon
Beef	10 lb.
Beets	7 lb.
Bread	2½ loaves
Butter	1 lb.
Cabbage for slaw	5 lb.
Cakes	2
Carrots	8 lb.
Cauliflower	4 lb.
Cheese	1 lb.
Chicken Pieces	50 pieces
Coffee	1 lb.
Cream	1 qt.
Fruit cocktail	2 to 2.5 qt.
Fruit juice	1 liter
Fruit salad	5 qt.
Ham/boneless	10 lb.
Hamburger	10 lb.
Hot dogs	4.5 lb.
Ice cream	1½ gallons
Lettuce	5 heads
Meat loaf	6 lb.
Milk	4 qt. or 1 gallon
Nuts	1 lb.
Olives	¼ lb.
Oysters/unshucked	6 qt.
Pickles	½ qt.

Pies	4
Potatoes	8.5 lb.
Potato salad	3 qt.
Potatoes/Scalloped	3 gallons
Roast pork	10 lb.
Rolls	25 to 50
Salad dressing	1 qt.
Sugar	½ lb.
Soup	1½ gallons
Tomato juice	1 liter
Vegetable salad	5 qt.
Whipping cream	1 pint

Picnic and Lunch Box Tip!
Don't leave food out at
temperatures between 40°
and 140°F for more than
2 hours (1 hour if the
temperature outside is over
90°F).
They may spoil.

Index

INDEX

16178193R00071

Made in the USA
Middletown, DE
09 December 2014